To My Valentine,
My Friend &
My Sweetheart

From Christy
With Love

2/14/91

Flavia

Until You
copyright © 1994 by Flavia Weedn
All rights reserved. Printed in Hong Kong.

For information write Andrews and McMeel,
a Universal Press Syndicate Company,
4900 Main Street, Kansas City, Missouri 64112

ISBN: 0-8362-4726-4

UNTIL YOU

Written and Illustrated
By Flavia Weedn

I

was

alone with

my dreams

until

you.

I

was

alone in

a crowd

FLAVIA

until

you.

Then,

in some

magical

way

GIANT

FIREWORK

ASSORTMENT

CAUTION: FLAMMABLE

FLAVIA

within

life's mystery,

we met.

you

became

my friend,

my love,

and the one

who brings me

Camelot.

you are the

place I run

to when I'm

frightened

and you

are the one

who shares

my dreams.

I

was

alone

and

my heart

was empty

*for I
never knew
the magic of love...*

until

you.

Flavia at work in her Santa Barbara studio

Flavia Weedn is a writer, painter and philosopher. Her life's work is about hope for the human spirit. "I want to reach people of all ages who have never been told, 'wait a minute, look around you. It's wonderful to be alive and every one of us matters. We can make a difference if we keep trying and never give up.'" It is Flavia's and her family's wish to awaken this spirit in each and every one of us. Flavia's messages are translated into many foreign languages on giftware, books and paper goods around the world.

To find out more about Flavia write to:
Flavia Publishing, Inc.
740 State Street, 3rd Floor
Santa Barbara, CA 93101 USA
or call: 805-564-6909